WHY VAMPIRE BATS SUCK BLOOD

and Other Gross Facts about Animals

by Jody Sullivan Rake

Consultant: Tanya Dewey, PhD
University of Michigan Museum of Zoology, Ann Arbor, Michigan

CAPSTONE PRESS
a capstone imprint

Library of Congress Cataloging-in-Publication Data
Rake, Jody Sullivan.
Why vampire bats suck blood and other gross facts about animals/by Jody
Sullivan Rake.
    p. cm.—(First facts: gross me out!)
 Includes bibliographical references and index.
 Summary: "Describes unusual behavior of animals, including vultures, hippos,
parrots, and hagfish"—Provided by publisher.
 ISBN 978-1-4296-7611-3 (library binding)
 ISBN 978-1-4296-7957-2 (paperback)
 1. Animal behavior—Miscellanea—Juvenile literature. I. Title.
 QL751.5.R35 2012
 591.5—dc23   2011035904

Editorial Credits

Lori Shores, editor; Veronica Correia, designer; Marcie Spence, media researcher;
    Kathy McColley, production specialist

Image Credits

Alamy: Blickwinkel, 13, Brandon Cole Marine Photography, 11, John Cancalosi, 16,
Poelzer Wolfgang, 21; Ardea: Adrian Warren, 5; Brandon D. Cole, 10; Minden Pictures:
Marijn Heuts, 19; Shutterstock: Aleksandr Kurganov, 8, Art_man, cover, Dr. Morley
Read, 18, edography, 12, Francois Loubser, 7, Hannamariah, 9, Nagel Photography, 15,
p.schwarz, 6, Reistlin Magere, 20, Roberto Cerruti, cover (background), Rusty Dodson,
17, Sz Akos, 3, 14, Virinaflora, 13 (cartoon), Yayayoyo, 5 (cartoon)

Printed in the United States of America in North Mankato, Minnesota.

102011   006405CGS12

TABLE OF CONTENTS

That's So Gross!

Animals are amazing creatures. They have some surprising ways of playing, hunting, and surviving. But animals also do some pretty gross things. Come and explore some of the animal world's yuckiest behaviors. Get ready to be grossed out!

Vampire Bats Love the Sight of Blood

Most bats eat bugs and fruits. Not vampire bats. They got their name for a good reason. These bats really do eat blood. Vampire bats bite the ankles of cows, horses, and other **mammals**. When the animals start to bleed, the bats lick the blood. But don't worry! The animals they bite don't become vampires.

mammal—a warm-blooded animal that breathes air and has hair or fur

Gross Fact!

Some other animals eat blood too.
But vampire bats don't eat anything
else. They live on just blood alone.

Vultures Stink!

Vultures have a useful but nasty trick. These large birds live in hot, dry areas. But they can't sweat to cool down. Instead, they poop all over their own legs. As the watery poop dries, it cools the vultures' legs.

Gross Fact!

Vultures have a gross diet too. They eat dead, rotting animals. Yuk!

How Much Does Your Parrot Love You?

How would you like a **vomit** valentine? Like many birds, parrots throw up food for their young to eat. But parrots also do it to show affection! Parrots vomit on their **mates**, babies, and other birds they love.

vomit—to throw up food and liquid from one's stomach through one's mouth
mate—the male or female partner of a pair of animals

Gross Fact!

Pet parrots will vomit on their human owners too. Sometimes they'll even throw up on their favorite toys!

Hagfish Are Such Slimeballs!

When it comes to gross sea animals, the hagfish wins. The eel-like hagfish eats dead animals from the inside out. But it's their **defense** that makes them really gross. When threatened, hagfish ooze gobs of slime from their skin. They're then able to slip away from their enemies.

defense—an ability to protect oneself from harm

Angry, Angry Hippos

Plant-eating hippos look friendly, but they can be grouchy. These giants fiercely guard their water holes and their young. If another hippo gets too close, they aim their rear ends and fire! They spray pee and poop, spinning their tails to splatter the mess everywhere. Stay back!

Giraffes and Their Talented Tongues

The tallest animal in the world also has one of the longest tongues. An adult giraffe's tongue can be 18 to 20 inches (46 to 51 centimeters) long. And its tongue is blue-black—not red! That tongue helps a giraffe reach the highest leaves on the African savannas. It also uses its tongue to clean out its dusty nose! Eeew!

savanna—a flat, grassy area of land with few or no trees

Gross Fact!

A long tongue needs a lot of spit to keep it wet. Giraffes drool almost all the time.

Horned Lizards Squirt What from Where?

Horned lizards puff out their spiny skin when they're threatened. But if a hungry animal creeps close to a horned lizard, watch out! This **reptile** will shoot blood out of its eyes. The blood can fly as far as 3 feet (0.9 meter). That will stop the enemy in its tracks!

reptile—a cold-blooded animal that breathes air and has a backbone

Gross Fact!

Horned lizards are often called horned toads because of their short, round bodies.

What's in an Owl Pellet?

You think vomit is gross? Check out owl **pellets**. Night-hunting owls eat mice, squirrels, and other small animals whole. But owls can't **digest** the bones, fur, and claws. Later the owl will throw up a yucky 2- to 4-inch (5- to 10-cm) clump of these animal pieces.

pellet—a mass of undigested hair, fur, and bones vomited by an owl

digest—to break down food so it can be used by the body

Sea Cucumbers Really Spill Their Guts

Sea cucumbers are soft, squishy sea animals. They have no teeth, claws, or shells for protection. But they do have a defense, and it's a doozy. They can squeeze their **intestines** out of their backsides into an attacker's face! The enemy gets a snack while the sea cucumber crawls away.

intestine—a long tube below the stomach that digests food and absorbs liquids

Gross Fact!

It takes about two weeks for a sea cucumber's intestines to grow back.

GLOSSARY

defense (di-FENS)—an ability to protect oneself from harm

digest (dy-JEST)—to break down food so it can be used by the body

intestine (in-TESS-tin)—a long tube below the stomach that digests food and absorbs liquids

mammal (MAM-uhl)—a warm-blooded animal that breathes air and has hair or fur; female mammals feed milk to their young

mate (MATE)—the male or female partner of a pair of animals

pellet (PEL-it)—a mass of undigested hair, fur, and bones vomited by an owl

reptile (REP-tile)—a cold-blooded animal that breathes air and has a backbone; most reptiles have scales

savanna (suh-VAN-uh)—a flat, grassy area of land with few or no trees

vomit (VOM-it)—to throw up food and liquid from one's stomach through one's mouth

READ MORE

Hanna, Jack. *The Wackiest, Wildest, Weirdest Animals in the World.* Nashville: Thomas Nelson, 2009.

Polydoros, Lori. *Strange but True Animals.* Strange but True. Mankato, Minn.: Capstone Press, 2011.

Seuling, Barbara. *Cows Sweat Through Their Noses: And Other Freaky Facts about Animal Habits, Characteristics, and Homes.* Freaky Facts. Minneapolis: Picture Window Books, 2008.

INTERNET SITES

FactHound offers a safe, fun way to find Internet sites related to this book. All of the sites on FactHound have been researched by our staff.

Here's all you do:

Visit *www.facthound.com*

Type in this code: 9781429676113

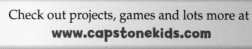
Super-cool stuff!

Check out projects, games and lots more at
www.capstonekids.com

INDEX

24